ONE LAND, MANY NATIONS

CHEROKEE NATION

BY TRACI SORELL

ART BY JESSE HUMMINGBIRD

Welcome to the CHEROKEE NATION

While many people think of the United States as one country and one land, it is actually a land made up of many nations.

Native American Nations currently exist in the lands called the United States.

And they've been here long before the United States became a country. These are sovereign nations with their own laws. Their citizens have dual citizenship—in their nation and in the United States. These nations have a rich history and culture that continues to today.

Let's learn about one of these nations, the Cherokee Nation, from tribally enrolled citizen Traci Sorell.

OSIYO!

Welcome to the Cherokee Nation, located among the wooded green hills of northeastern Oklahoma.

In the following pages, we'll explore the **history of the Cherokee Nation**—the largest tribe in the United States. We'll examine how its **tribal government** works. Then we'll see what **daily life** is like for Cherokee people. We'll also meet some important Cherokee citizens you should know. Finally, we'll wrap up our tour with a traditional Cherokee story.

You'll find **large lakes, rural towns, winding rivers, gravel roads, small cities,** and some of the friendliest people you'll ever meet. More than 380,000 citizens make up the Cherokee Nation. About 141,000 of them live within the tribe's fourteen-county area. The rest live in other parts of Oklahoma and all around the world.

LOCATION

But first, let's head to Tahlequah, Oklahoma.

That's where the Cherokee Nation capital is located.

Today you can visit Tahlequah and see the former National Capitol building, now the Cherokee National History Museum, and the historic Cherokee National Jail downtown.

Tahlequah wasn't always the Cherokee Nation's capital. The federal government forcibly removed the Cherokee people from their homelands in the southeastern United States in the late 1830s. Once they arrived in what was then called Indian Territory, tribal leaders needed to reestablish the government in their new location. On September 6, 1839, they voted on a new constitution to govern the Cherokee people. That is when they named Tahlequah their capital.

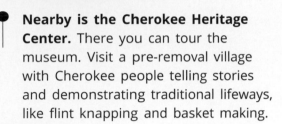

- **Nearby is the Cherokee Heritage Center.** There you can tour the museum. Visit a pre-removal village with Cherokee people telling stories and demonstrating traditional lifeways, like flint knapping and basket making.

- You'll also see post-removal life in an **1890s rural village**. There you can step inside the one-room schoolhouse, general store, log cabin, and smokehouse.

TRAVELING TO

TAHLEQUAH, OKLAHOMA

Where to Go

Visit **Seminary Hall**, the oldest (and maybe haunted) building on the Northeastern State University campus. It was built in 1889 to educate Cherokee women, then the state purchased it in 1909 to create a college.

The Cherokee Spider Gallery features a variety of arts and crafts made by talented Cherokee artisans, located downtown by the Cherokee National History Museum.

Foods to Try

Enjoy Indian tacos and frybread at the **River City Cafe**, right inside the Cherokee Casino.

For the best, most affordable street tacos around, head to **Jose's Mexican Restaurant**.

HISTORY AT-A-GLANCE

Now you know where the Cherokee Nation and its people are located. Let's explore their history prior to removal to Indian Territory, which later became the state of Oklahoma.

The ancestors of today's Cherokee Nation citizens originally lived in the southeastern United States.

They lived over a large area where the states of Tennessee, Kentucky, Virginia, North Carolina, South Carolina, Alabama, and Georgia come together.

Their lives were organized around clan and ritual. Each Cherokee person belonged to their mother's clan, making one's maternal relatives very important in a child's upbringing and teaching. But clan relatives might also be adopted from other tribes. So, not everyone was a blood relative. Still, no one could marry within the same clan.

Historically, women owned all the land and took care of the crops. Men hunted deer and small game. Everyone in the village or town followed a rich ceremonial life through daily rituals as well as seasonal celebrations. Whether the women were preparing the field to plant or harvest, or the men primed themselves to leave on a hunt or fight a battle, they performed ceremonies to ready them for each task or event in their lives. This sounds very different than how life is lived today, doesn't it?

Cherokee people also lived in villages or larger towns. These had local leaders rather than having one centralized government like they do now. These local leaders, the Peace Chief and the War Chief, were chosen through the clan system. They met in the seven-sided council house with representatives from each of the seven clans. There they discussed and solved issues facing the people. The Peace Chief oversaw ceremonial and day-to-day village life. The War Chief handled all outside business: trade, negotiations, and warfare. Clan mothers also played an important role in each village's decision-making process.

Don't miss Diligwa, Cherokee Village in 1710.

Make sure to take a tour at the Cherokee Heritage Center of Diligwa, a typical 1710 village where today's Cherokee people share how our ancestors lived together at the time of increasing trade with Europeans.

Next we'll see how the Europeans' invasion of Cherokee homelands disrupted this way of life. Between the 1540 visit of Hernando de Soto from Spain and an influx of British traders a little over a hundred years later, the Cherokee began to see more and more Europeans in their villages. These visitors brought diseases with them. This caused the death of many Cherokee people who had no immunity.

The Europeans also fought among themselves over land and resources. This often forced the Cherokee people to divide and take sides in battle. The Cherokee who survived this turmoil found that Europeans were going to stay. These outsiders started the process of colonization. Colonization occurs when a group of people settle among the Indigenous people of an area to control them and their land. This happened to the Cherokee Nation.

The colonists demanded the Cherokee people change how they lived, governed, and even maintained their ceremonial life.

They also wanted Cherokee land, resources, and gold. The colonists formed a national government separate from the European countries they came from. For the Cherokee, this meant their Nation now existed within the new nation of the United States. But Cherokee people were not U.S. citizens.

It's hard to imagine how the Cherokee people continued after losing so many to disease and warfare and seeing their Nation surrounded by the United States. But they did. And their way of life changed forever. Cherokee leaders no longer governed at the village or town level, where clans chose their own Peace and War Chiefs, but instead across a region. These leaders had to sign many treaties, or legal agreements, with European leaders. They had to continually show which land was theirs and which land the colonists could live on.

Eventually, the Cherokee even adopted the same three branches of government as the United States: executive, legislative, and judicial. Many Cherokee adopted Christian beliefs after European missionaries from various churches worked to convert them from their traditional ceremonial life. Cherokee people did all this in hopes that their Nation could remain in its homeland. Yet, their actions were not enough.

White settlers still wanted more Cherokee land. Because of this, the United States government decided that, although a small number of Cherokee had moved west, the majority now needed to go too.

This caused a major split between Cherokee leaders when some signed the removal treaty and others opposed it. Regardless of how Cherokee people felt about the treaty, the U.S. military rounded up Cherokee elders, mothers, fathers, and children. They placed the Cherokee in detention camps before sending them to Indian Territory. At least 2,000 Cherokees died before leaving camp because of the unsanitary conditions. Then, from late summer in 1838 through March 24, 1839, when the last of the Cherokee arrived, another 2,000 lost their lives. They died on what the Cherokee remember as the "Trail Where They Cried"—the forced migration to Indian Territory. While a few thousand traveled via ferry on southern waterways, some Cherokee people traveled on foot or by horse. Some went along a northern route and ran into snow and an icy Mississippi River.

Despite the split between tribal leaders and the hardships endured on the Trail of Tears, the Cherokee Nation reestablished its government in Indian Territory. Doing so took many years of working through conflict, including the U.S. Civil War. But at the end of the 1800s, the U.S. federal government had a new challenge for the Cherokee Nation. The U.S. decided to allot, or divide up, the Cherokee Nation's shared land into individual parcels for each Cherokee citizen. Receiving allotments also made the Cherokee people citizens of the United States. When Oklahoma became a state on November 16, 1907, the new state did not recognize tribal governments and their courts as having jurisdiction over their tribal citizens. That meant state law governed Cherokee people, not Cherokee laws or leaders. Also, many Cherokee people lost their land due to taxation and sales in 1908 after statehood.

ART
TRAIL OF TEARS

Life-size sculptures depicting the cross-country trail on which more than 2,000 Cherokee people perished more than 160 years ago are on display at the Cherokee Heritage Center in Tahlequah, Oklahoma. The faces on the sculptures are modeled after Cherokee citizens.

TRIBAL GOVERNMENT TODAY

Tough history to read, huh? It is not easy to learn about all the hardships Cherokee people faced in the past. It's even harder for Cherokee citizens to know that their ancestors endured that pain and loss. Thankfully, Cherokee people are resilient.

The path forward for the Cherokee Nation was not easy after statehood. Even though the state of Oklahoma did not recognize them, Cherokee leaders continued to meet, exercise their power to the extent they could, and offer support to their citizens.

They maintained a relationship with the federal government. Cherokee people also worked to maintain their language and ceremonial life, even though it was difficult to do so. Over time, federal laws and policies changed to allow Cherokee and other tribal leaders in Oklahoma to regain more control over their own affairs.

Today, the Cherokee Nation works hard to protect and exercise its sovereignty.

Sovereignty means the right to govern the people and land under its jurisdiction. The Cherokee Nation's sovereignty has existed since before the Europeans arrived on the continent. Cherokee Nation citizens age eighteen and older—regardless of where they live—can register to vote. They can elect the Principal Chief, Deputy Chief, and Tribal Council members to take care of the tribe's governmental responsibilities. The Principal Chief appoints and the Tribal Council confirms the judges serving on the Cherokee Nation's District Court and Supreme Court.

The tribal leaders also consult directly with the U.S. president, other agencies in the executive branch, and the U.S. Congress about federal laws and policies that affect the tribe.

The Cherokee Nation's elected officials also represent the tribe in Oklahoma City when proposed Oklahoma state laws might benefit or hurt the Cherokee Nation. The tribe works closely with the state's county governments within its reservation borders. They partner in several areas to maintain infrastructure such as rural waterlines, roads, and bridge construction.

The Cherokee Nation also provides additional money to public schools that Cherokee children attend. One part of the tribal government's mission is to improve "the quality of life" for Cherokee citizens now and in the future. No small task to accomplish with so many citizens, right?

Native American chiefs visiting **President Grant** in the White House, 1871

President Calvin Coolidge is presented with a copy of *The Red Man in the United States: A Survey of the Present Day American Indian*, by Ruth Muskrat, a Cherokee Nation citizen, 1923.

President Barack Obama with Cherokee Nation citizen Kimberly Teehee, his Senior Policy Advisor for Native American Affairs, 2012

President George W. Bush, far right, prepares to hear the Cherokee National Youth Choir, in the East Room of the White House during an event honoring the opening of the National Museum of the American Indian, 2004.

DAILY LIFE TODAY

Cherokee Nation Reservation

Stretched across fourteen counties, the Cherokee Nation covers most of the northeastern corner in what is now Oklahoma. After the forced removal of the Cherokee people from their eastern homelands, they arrived in what was then Indian Territory and moved on to the ancestral lands of the Osage Nation.

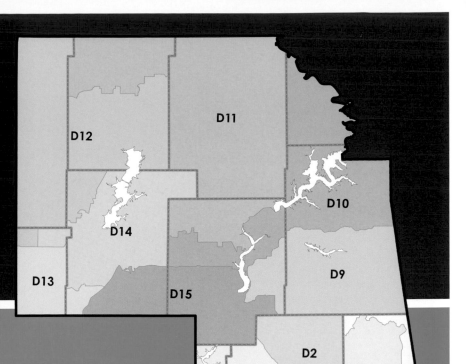

Part of the Cherokee Nation's focus is on providing its citizens access to health care, homes, education, and jobs.

The tribe has built many health care clinics across the reservation. This allows tribal citizens to find medical help closer to home. There are also programs that the Cherokee Nation runs to help fix homes and build new ones that tribal citizens can buy. In addition to providing extra money to local schools, the tribe also runs its own Pre-K through sixth- grade language immersion school and a combined school for seventh- through twelfth-grade students. Also, eligible Cherokee citizens—whether or not they live within the area of jurisdiction—can apply for college scholarships.

Each Labor Day weekend, the Cherokee Nation celebrates the signing of the 1839 constitution during its Cherokee National Holiday in Tahlequah.

Just over one-third of the Cherokee Nation's citizens live on the reservation. There one sees the economic impact of the jobs created through the Nation's various industries. Separate from the tribal government, Cherokee Nation Businesses is a for-profit company. It operates in many areas. Some of these include real estate, manufacturing, delivery of goods, telecommunications, engineering, information technology, and hospitality, such as hotels, restaurants, and casinos. These provide jobs for both Cherokee and non-Cherokee people.

But some of the most important work that the tribal government does is reflected in its mission statement: "preserving and promoting Cherokee culture, language, and values." The Cherokee Nation now offers a variety of programs and services in person and online for its citizens, regardless of where they live.

More than 60,000 people attend the Cherokee National Holiday, each Labor Day weekend. If you attend, you'll be able to watch traditional game competitions, such as a cornstalk shoot and Cherokee marbles. There are softball and golf tournaments, too. You can also enjoy storytelling, the Principal Chief's State of the Nation address, a parade, a children's fishing derby, arts and crafts, live music, a variety of Cherokee foods, and an intertribal powwow.

Throughout the year, the Cherokee Nation offers classes on traditional arts, games, and tribal history across the fourteen counties as well as in cities around the U.S. where large numbers of Cherokee citizens live. Cherokee language classes are available free online.

Cherokee elders are teaching younger generations the language, traditional games, and the arts.

This allows those learning to pass on the knowledge to the next generation and keep the traditions going. The tribe honors those who have outstanding knowledge of Cherokee art forms and cultural practices and are committed to preserving or reviving them. Those Cherokee citizens chosen for this award are named Cherokee National Treasures.

Like most of you reading this book, Cherokee children attend public schools and participate in sports and other after-school activities. They also benefit from the tribe's ability to offer special culture and language programs beyond what is taught at home. Each summer, the Cherokee Nation offers a free weeklong overnight camp for teenage citizens focusing on science, technology, engineering, art, and math. The tribe offers summer cultural day camps for younger citizens, too. Cherokee young people can also try out for the Cherokee National Youth Choir, and children can compete to represent the tribe as Little Cherokee Ambassadors. These opportunities to learn, experience, and practice Cherokee culture and language will help even the youngest citizens to continue teaching traditions to future generations.

Each spring and fall, the Cherokee Heritage Center welcomes school groups just like yours to visit and play traditional games like chunkey and stickball. You'll even learn a few words like tsalagi (JAH-lah-ghee) which means "Cherokee" and yona (YO-nah) which means "bear." You'll get to hear Cherokee stories, some funny and others a little spooky. If you can't make it to the Cherokee Heritage Center with your school group, you're still welcome to visit anytime!

RULES OF THE GAME

STICKBALL

Historically, stickball was not played as a sport. Cherokee men played stickball to settle serious disputes among their villages or against men from other southeastern tribes. Today, most Cherokee children and adults play a social version at ceremonial grounds and in some communities. Players score points by flinging a handmade ball covered in deer hide to hit a carved wooden ball or fish perched atop a 25-foot cedar pole to score points. Female players use their hands instead of sticks that male players must use. Teams decide the game's duration by agreeing to play a determined amount of time or by which team scores a certain number of points first.

STORIES

Wado for learning about the Cherokee Nation, its history, culture, and citizens! We'll finish your tour with a traditional story about how the Milky Way came to be.

The Origin of the Milky Way

Some people in the south had a corn mill,
in which they pounded the corn into meal,
and several mornings when they came to fill it
they noticed that some of the meal had been stolen during the night.
They examined the ground and found the tracks of a dog,
so the next night they watched,
and when the dog came from the north
and began to eat the meal out of the bowl
they sprang out and whipped him.
He ran off howling to his home in the north,
with the meal dropping from his mouth as he ran,
and leaving behind a white trail where now
we see the Milky Way, which the Cherokee call to this day
gili utsun stanunyi (ghee-LEE oot-soon stan-UNH-yee),
"where the dog ran."

—As told in 1888 by Swimmer (1835–1899), a Cherokee storyteller

FAMOUS CITIZENS

Osda! Now that you know more about the Cherokee Nation, its history, and culture, let's introduce you to some of its more well-known historical and contemporary citizens.

Nanyehi

The most famous Cherokee woman in the colonial era is Nanyehi (later known as Nancy Ward, who lived from about 1738–1824). She hailed from the Wolf Clan, the protectors of the Cherokee people and clan of the War Chiefs. She fought in her husband's place after he was killed in a battle against the Muscogee (Creek) Nation. Nanyehi's bravery earned her the distinction of Beloved Woman among the Cherokee. This allowed her to speak at Cherokee Council meetings and to pardon, condemn, or release any captive held by the tribe.

Sequoyah

After Nanyehi, Sequoyah (~1770–1843) is the most famous Cherokee man in the historical era. Sequoyah lived in the same general area as Nanyehi, worked as a silversmith, and spoke only Cherokee while growing up. He is best known for creating a written language for the Cherokee people. He developed eighty-six characters to represent each syllable in the Cherokee language. He then taught the syllabary to the Cherokee people.

The Cherokee Nation officially adopted Sequoyah's syllabary in 1825 and still teaches it today. Sequoyah's writing invention allowed a tribal newspaper, *The Cherokee Phoenix*, to be created and printed in Cherokee and English in 1828. You can visit Sequoyah's cabin, where he lived in Indian Territory after removal. You can also see a statue of him in the U.S. Capitol building in Washington, D.C.

The historic Will Rogers Birthplace Museum in Oologah.

Will Rogers

Most people have heard of Will Rogers (1879–1935), a popular Cherokee actor, writer, and philosopher. Born in Indian Territory after the removal, Will grew up on his family's ranch. A freed enslaved man taught him to rope and ride. Will did not enjoy school and often missed classes. He preferred to be on the ranch or a cattle drive. Later, he left home and used his trick roping skills and quick wit to entertain people all over the world. Will starred in movies, wrote books, and drafted columns for newspapers and magazines.

He is best known for his quotes about everyday life and politics, including how the Cherokee and other tribes were mistreated by the Europeans. Like Sequoyah, Will Rogers has a statue in the U.S. Capitol building in Washington, D.C. You can visit his boyhood home, museum, and memorial in northeastern Oklahoma.

Mary Golda Ross

Someone you may not have heard of but you definitely should know about is Mary Golda Ross (1908–2008). Mary was the first known Native American female engineer in the United States. Unlike Will, Mary loved school—especially learning about math. She grew up in the Cherokee Nation after Oklahoma became a state. Mary went to college at age sixteen and taught high school math after graduation.

She continued studying for her master's degree while working. When the United States entered World War II in 1941, Mary wanted to help the entire country. So, she moved to California and went to work for a large company that made fighter planes and rockets. Mary also studied to be an aerospace engineer to help people travel to space. Most of her work is classified, meaning it is top secret and cannot be known to everyone. It is well known that Mary helped many other Native Americans and women in general become engineers, scientists, and mathematicians during her lifetime.

Painting by Cherokee artist America Meredith

JOHN ROSS
1790 – 1866
PRINCIPAL CHIEF
OF THE
CHEROKEE NATION
1828 – 1866

Wilma Mankiller

The most famous Cherokee in recent history is Wilma Mankiller (1945–2010), the first woman to serve as Principal Chief of the Cherokee Nation. Born on her father's allotment in northeastern Oklahoma, Wilma moved with her family to San Francisco, California, when she was eleven years old. She met families from other tribes who had also moved to find better jobs through the federal government's voluntary relocation program in the 1950s. She saw people taking action in the civil rights movement and tribes in California exercising their sovereignty. This experience spurred her to return home, where she felt she could use her education and skills to help the Cherokee Nation. She served as Principal Chief for ten years and focused on health care, community needs, and education for Cherokee people.

LANGUAGE.

Osiyo [OH-see-yo] = Hello

Osda [OHS-dah] = Good/Great

Nanyehi [Nahn-yay-hee] = Nancy Ward

Wado [WAH-doe] = Thank you

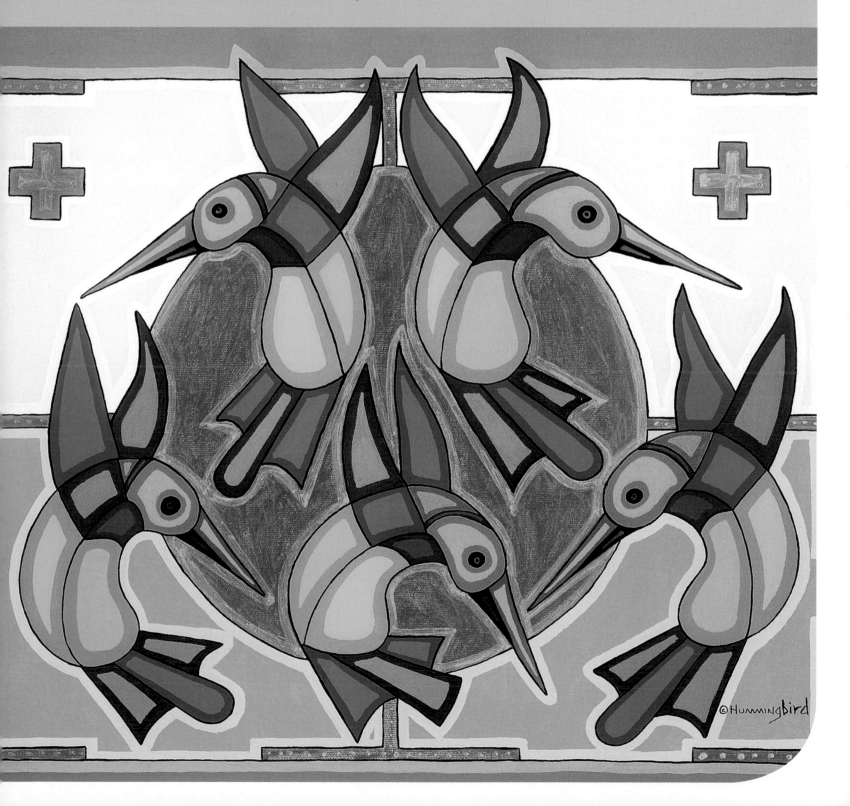

BIBLIOGRAPHY

Websites

Cherokee Nation, "Mission Statement https://www.cherokee.org/#:~:text=MISSION%3A,generations%20of%20Cherokee%20Nation%20citizens (accessed February 9, 2020).

Clara Sue Kidwell, "Allotment," *The Encyclopedia of Oklahoma History and Culture*, https://www.okhistory.org/publications/enc/entry.php?entry=AL011 (accessed February 9, 2020).

U.S. National Park Service, "Nunahi-Duna-Dlo-Hilu-I" — Trail Where They Cried," *Fort Smith National Historic Site*, https://www.nps.gov/fosm/learn/historyculture/nunahi-duna-dlo-hilu-i-trail-where-they-cried.htm (accessed February 9, 2020).

Linda D. Wilson, "Statehood Movement," *The Encyclopedia of Oklahoma History and Culture*, https://www.okhistory.org/publications/enc/entry.php?entry=ST025 (accessed February 9, 2020).

Books

Conley, Robert J. *The Cherokee Nation: A History*. Albuquerque: University of New Mexico Press, 2005.

Mankiller, Wilma, and Michael Wallis. *Mankiller: A Chief and Her People*. New York: St. Martin's Press, 1993.

Mooney, James. *History, Myths, and Sacred Formulas of the Cherokees*. Asheville, NC: Historical Images, 1992.

For more information on the Cherokee Nation:

Cherokee Nation: www.cherokee.org

Cherokee Nation Tourism: www.visitcherokeenation.com

Cherokee Nation Businesses: www.cherokeenationbusinesses.com

MEET TRACi

Cherokee Nation citizen and award-winning author Traci Sorell writes fiction and nonfiction in a variety of formats for children and teens. Her debut nonfiction picture book, *We Are Grateful: Otsaliheliga,* shares a contemporary Cherokee view of gratitude across the four seasons—beginning in fall with the Cherokee New Year.

A former federal Indian law attorney and advocate, Traci lives with her family on the Cherokee Nation reservation in northeastern Oklahoma, where she was born and spent most of her childhood.

MEET LEE.

Dr. Lee Francis IV is a Laguna Pueblo decendent on his father's side, through his grandmother Ethel and great-grandmother Agnes. He is the founder of Native Realities Press, a publishing company dedicated to creating comic books by and about Native Americans. He also owns and runs a bookstore called Red Planet Books and Comics, and started the first Indigenous Comic Con.

MYTH-BUSTING

Q: Do all Indians live in teepees? What do the Laguna people live in?

A: No. Laguna people live in buildings that could be called the first apartments. Their traditional dwellings are multi-family houses that are often two or more stories. These dwellings are made of stone and adobe, a kind of mud/clay/concrete developed by Pueblo people as an important building material. They also have what could be considered "modern" homes made of concrete, metal, and wood. Ultimately, Laguna people live in many types of homes.

Q: Do Lagunas wear costumes at their Feast Day dances?

A: There are many parts of clothing used but they are not a costume. The cultural dress is called regalia. A costume often means that someone is playing dress-up. For Laguna people the traditional clothing has often been hand-crafted and possibly handed down over many generations and has a deep cultural meaning for the wearer.

Q: Do Laguna wear headdresses?

A: No. Headdresses are a cultural element for many Native American peoples but not for Lagunas. Laguna people do use feathers for some cultural activities but not the headdress that is seen in movies and TV.

Q: How do I learn more about Laguna?

A: You can visit their website: https://www.lagunapueblo-nsn.gov.

LANGUAGE.

The people of the Pueblo of Laguna speak a language called Keres.

The language is spoken at eight other Pueblos in New Mexico. Keres is a *language isolate*, which means that it is not connected to any other languages in the world.

Like many Indigenous languages, Keres is a place-based language. That means that the focus of the language is on location and context, rather than object-based, like many Western languages, that focus on things and vocabulary.

Keres is also an endangered language. There are very few fluent speakers still alive. However, the Pueblo of Laguna has been doing many things to revitalize the language. It has had great success in many of its programs in teaching the language to a new generation.

Maintaining and promoting an Indigenous language, like Keres, is important because it helps the Laguna people connect to their culture and to their elders and ancestors. Many Laguna elders will remind young people to be aware of their words and to learn their language in order to be strong and take care of the Pueblo for future generations.

Leslie Marmon Silko

Leslie Marmon Silko is an author at the forefront of what has been called the Native American Renaissance. Her books focus on Native American life and challenge racism and colonialism.

Deb Haaland

Deb Haaland is a politician from New Mexico. She was one of the first two Native American women elected to the U.S. Congress. She now serves as United States Secretary of the Interior and is the first Native American to run this government department.

FAMOUS MEMBERS.

Many Laguna Pueblo have received national and international attention. Here are a few.

Frank Hudson

Frank Hudson was a football player and coach. He played for the Carlisle Indian Industrial School and was known for his outstanding kicking. Some say he was the greatest football kicker of all time. He was the first Native American football player named an All-American.

Michael Kanteena

Michael Kanteena is an award-winning potter known for pottery inspired by his ancestors. He continues to create and practice his craft to this day.

STORIES

Laguna Pueblo people have many stories. Here is a poem from Laguna Pueblo scholar and poet, Dr. Lee Francis III.

At the center of creation
I stand and bear witness
On this St. Ann's Day

At the edge of blue mountain
I raise my hands in thanks
to the mothers
    who have cared
    for the people
    who have cared
    for me
and I sing an honor song
    to our mother
and I sing an honor song
    to our sisters
and I sing an honor song
and I sing an honor song.

The people of Laguna are not relics of the past. They are not the Native Americans you often see in movies or television shows and riding horses chasing cowboys. They are everyday individuals with a strong and lasting culture. They are mothers and fathers, grandfathers and grandmothers. They are veterans and teachers, doctors and lawyers. They are students and professors. They are culture keepers and storytellers. They are taxi drivers and sailors, artists and musicians.

They bring knowledge and expertise. They bring history and humor. They bring tradition and technology.

Some speak their language. Some do not. Some grew up in Laguna. Some did not. Some live on the Laguna reservation. Some live in faraway lands. But no matter their education, their jobs, their hobbies, or their backgrounds, they have pride in themselves and their community. They see a bright future for their children and their Pueblo. They are Ishkay Hanu, One People.

Jessica "Jaylyn" Atsye, Melissa Sanchez (Laguna and Acoma), and Emmett Shkeme Garcia of Laguna Pueblo, talk about the importance of the "Rock Your Mocs" campaign during a celebration at the Indian Pueblo Cultural Center in Albuquerque, New Mexico.

MODERN LIFE

The population of Laguna citizens is almost 8,000. Only about half live at home on the reservation.

Many Lagunas reside in cities through the United States. Many Laguna people are world travelers. Sometimes their jobs take them to different places, but they are still Laguna citizens.

A number of Lagunas work for the **federal government**. This means they live in places like Albuquerque, New Mexico or Washington D.C. Many Lagunas serve in the **military**. This means they live in different countries or even at sea. Many Lagunas are students who go to colleges and **universities** around the world while they are working on their degrees.

There are Laguna people everywhere. From North to South and East to West. You never know when you might meet a Laguna person in the world, but they are out there.

Justice Raquel Montoya-Lewis was appointed to the Washington State Supreme Court by Governor Jay Inslee in December 2019.

IN THE WORLD.

The Laguna people live in many states and
countries.

Tom Dailey, a WWII veteran from the Laguna Pueblo in New Mexico, sings a memorial song at the Red Earth Native American Festival.

VETERANS. AND SERVICE

Throughout the history of Native Americans in the United States, military service has been very important. From the Revolutionary War to Iraq and Afghanistan, Native American service men and women have played very important roles in the victories of the U.S. Military.

Laguna is no different.

Laguna men (and later women) have served in every modern combat action in every branch of the U.S. Armed Forces. Many elders continue to tell stories of their or their family members' service in World War II as well as the other military actions of the United States.

Today, there are a number of Laguna veterans and service men and women who are serving honorably in the U.S. Armed Forces. Many of these people are second, third, and fourth generation soldiers. Memorial Day and Veterans Day are both important holidays at Laguna.

Scorpionweed (Phacelia sp.)

Rabbitbrush or Chamiso Blanco (Chrysothamnus Nauseosus)

Wild Four O'Clock or Maravilla (Mirabilis Multiflorum)

HEALING WITH LOCAL PLANT LIFE

The health and well-being of the community is essential to the Pueblo of Laguna.

Because of this, the Laguna leadership has made many efforts over the years to create programs and institutions that serve the health needs of the people. The Pueblo government has provided many resources to create and expand an Elder Care Center (Laguna Rainbow) and a division for health, social services, and athletics (Laguna Health and Wellness). Even the local industries play their part. Laguna Development Corporation has supported youth sports leagues and scholarships for a number of years.

There are also many Lagunas who practice traditional ways of healing. They use local plants and organics based on practices handed down through many generations. These traditional ways continue to be important cultural knowledge that has been maintained through the centuries. As many Lagunas have always known: a healthy community is a happy community.

Being located right off Interstate 40, makes it an easy stop for people making the journey across the U.S. In fact, **the church of St. Joseph, the original Catholic church built in 1699, can be seen from the highway**. It is perched atop a picturesque hill.

There are some rules, however, for tourists and travelers to recognize when they visit the Pueblo. One of the most important is that Laguna people actually live in the houses around the village plazas. They are not tourist attractions. They have a vibrant and wonderful history and many of the people **may** open their homes to friends and family during celebrations. But this is not an open invitation to everyone.

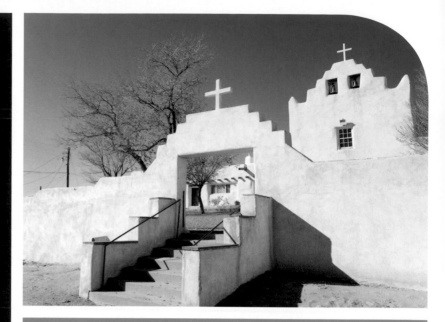

Further, photographs on the reservation are also not allowed. You may get permission from the Pueblo of Laguna Tribal Office to film in certain, designated places but cameras, and even sketches, are not allowed near the plaza or on Feast Days.

When in doubt, it is always a good rule of thumb for tourists and travelers alike to ask what is appropriate when being on the Laguna reservation.

TRAVEL AND TOURISM

Like many of the Pueblo villages throughout New Mexico, Laguna is often an exciting destination for travelers from around the world.

Their education would have revolved around stories, mentorship, observations, and guided practice. When the Spanish arrived in the 1500's, religious schools and day schools attempted to replace the traditional ways of educating children. In the late 1800's, Boarding Schools took Laguna children far away from their homes so they could be educated in a westernized system. These schools were very difficult for many Native American children, though some were quite successful and learned to adapt.

However, Laguna people always knew education was and continues to be very important to the success and well-being of the Pueblo. Laguna leadership created a scholarship program in 1962 and has supported many students in their efforts to get a college degree.

The Laguna Department of Education was established in 1991. It oversees more than 500 children from preschool through college.

The scholarship program continues to support Laguna citizens of all ages in attaining degrees. Laguna citizens have always valued education and will continue to do so for many years to come.

EDUCATION

In early times, education looked very different. Laguna children were taught important lessons by their families and community elders.

CITIZENSHIP

The Constitution of the Pueblo of Laguna outlines who is a citizen.

Citizenship is very important to all sovereign nations, including the Pueblo of Laguna. Sovereignty, or sovereign, means that the people get to make large and small choices for themselves and their community. The right to self-governance has been affirmed by treaties with the United States.

Citizenship for Laguna Pueblo people is determined by a system often called Blood Quantum or Degree of Indian Blood. In this system, Laguna citizens must meet a percentage requirement of Laguna heritage in order to be considered a citizen of the Pueblo. The requirements have changed over the past century but remain as a way for the Pueblo to determine who is a citizen.

Traditional Laguna drummers

Buffalo dance performed by residents from Laguna Pueblo on July 4th.

Pueblo men perform the Eagle Dance near the start of an electronics parts plant the tribe built in Laguna, New Mexico, 1963.

CELEBRATIONS

Laguna people have many celebrations throughout the year. From birthdays to Feast Days, the Pueblo finds many ways to bring family and community together to participate in cultural activities, laugh, and be festive.

Feast Days are celebrated among the six villages at certain cultural times during the year. The main Feast Days are March 19th and September 19th. They take place at the main village of Laguna. These Feast Days are marked with vendors, carnival rides, cultural dances, and religious activities. Families in all the villages will feed friends and relatives throughout the day. Many traditional foods will be prepared to remind Laguna citizens of their home and culture.

Other celebrations for birthdays, graduations, and holidays will also have traditional foods and activities that bring the people together in large and small ways. These celebrations are the ways in which Laguna people continue to show the world their joyous, kind, and resilient spirit—even in times of struggle.

Pueblo people have been growing foods throughout present day New Mexico for thousands of years.

Traditional foods included corn, beans, and squash and have been staples of Indigenous diets throughout the centuries.

Prior to the 1950's, the Pueblo of Laguna also had a number of fruit orchards throughout the villages.

Fresh wheat bread baked in an outdoor oven, called an horno, is a nutritious staple food. Venison, elk, wild turkey, and other game from hunts are included in meals for various ceremonies and celebrations. The traditional Laguna diet is a filling and balanced meal.

Today, Laguna people have a number of choices to add to their meals. The local grocery store provides many fresh fruits and vegetables and lots of items found at stores around the United States. Although some people have suffered poor health effects from diet choices high in sugar, the traditional foods have always been a healthy way to remain connected to the land and the culture.

FOOD.

The Laguna Development Corporation (LDC) was created to develop, oversee, and operate businesses at the Pueblo, including the Rt. 66 Resort and Casino.

This casino has provided many jobs and opportunities to Laguna people for more than two decades.

Entrepreneurship is also something Laguna value. Many Laguna citizens have opened successful businesses throughout the reservation. Many more serve in leadership positions throughout the world. Laguna has a number of investments and prospects to keep the community successful for many years to come.

DAILY LIFE TODAY: BUSINESS

Even before the entrance of the railroad, the people of Laguna have been smart business leaders. Trading with the Spanish, the Mexicans, and the Americans for several hundred years, has made Laguna into an economic powerhouse.

Many businesses and industries have helped bring jobs and goods to Laguna. These include the earliest trading posts, Laguna Industries, the Jackpile Mine, and many of the small businesses on the reservation that help create a strong community.

PUEBLO OF LAGUNA

In 1908, the Pueblo of Laguna adopted its first Constitution. It has been revised and amended several times over the past century to adapt to the changes in the Pueblo and the world.

The Constitution has served to unite the six villages under one system of government, rather than individual village governments.

The Laguna Constitution outlines leadership roles and responsibilities for the Pueblo of Laguna Council. It is made up of twenty-one members. Each village has two representatives (twelve total). The other nine positions are elected by the citizens of the Pueblo. **The Governor is the highest elected official of Laguna and has important cultural and operational responsibilities.** Though Council members have a good deal of authority, they are always aware that they are accountable to the people of Laguna. Their decisions are always for the well-being of the Pueblo and its people.

Today, the government of Laguna oversees many important activities for the well-being and success of the Pueblo. Education, health services, business, economic development, social services, and important cultural activities are all coordinated and supported by the government.

The village leadership also continues to play important roles for the people, especially for cultural and social needs throughout the year.

TRIBAL GOVERNMENT TODAY

In 1982, the mine stopped operations. This left many Laguna people without jobs. But the leadership of the Pueblo worked very hard. Over the next several years they created new opportunities for Laguna people through education, economic development, and smart investments.

After the mine closed in 1982, it went through a process called reclamation. That filled in the pit operations to return the land to its original state. This process took around seven years and continues to be monitored today.

JACKPILE MINE

While out tending his sheep in 1950, Diné shepherd Paddy Martinez came across a glowing rock. And with this, uranium was discovered in Western New Mexico. It would change the entire state, including Laguna.

Opened in 1953, Jackpile Mine (located near the village of Paguate) was operated by the Anaconda mining company. **At the time of operation, the Jackpile Mine was the largest open-pit uranium mine in the world.** It provided more nuclear material to the Cold War efforts than any other site in the United States.

As the United States expanded, the development of roads followed the train rail lines. When New Mexico became a state in 1912, transportation was very important to connect cities and towns, Laguna included. Now that New Mexico was a state, Laguna Pueblo officially became a reservation. A reservation is a designation of land within the United States where Native American nations govern, or rule, themselves. There are many reservations in the U.S. that were negotiated by treaties with the Federal Government.

In the early 1900's, automobiles began to replace railroads and wagons as the main method of transportation.

The idea for Route 66 was to connect all the smaller roads and backroads throughout the country into one "Mother Road" that stretched from Chicago to Los Angeles.

The "Mother Road" ran directly through the heart of Laguna. It brought many goods, services, and tourists along its path. The road continued to help Laguna be one of the most connected and active Pueblos in New Mexico. In the 1950's and 60's, Interstate 40 took over as the main roadway through Laguna, but Old Route 66 still connects the villages and many neighborhoods throughout the reservation.

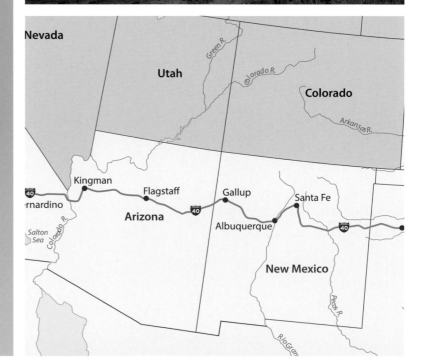

STATEHOOD AND RT. 66

Get your kicks on Route 66!

WORKING ON THE RAILROAD

In the late 1800's, the Atchison, Topeka, and Santa Fe (ATSF) Railroad Company wanted to continue their rail line through New Mexico.

Navigating through the canyons of central New Mexico was a difficult task. It took the company directly through Laguna Pueblo lands.

The leadership of Laguna was very smart. Knowing they had claim over the land, guaranteed to them under the Treaty of Guadalupe Hidalgo, they were able to negotiate the right of way to include jobs for Laguna people.

Those Laguna people worked on the rail lines and started new villages, called Colonies. These extended from New Mexico to California. These Colonies were boxcar villages where the Lagunas would live when they were working on the trains or rail lines.

To this day, many Laguna families still speak of their time in the Colonies. Only one Colony remains today: Albuquerque, where many Laguna people reside.

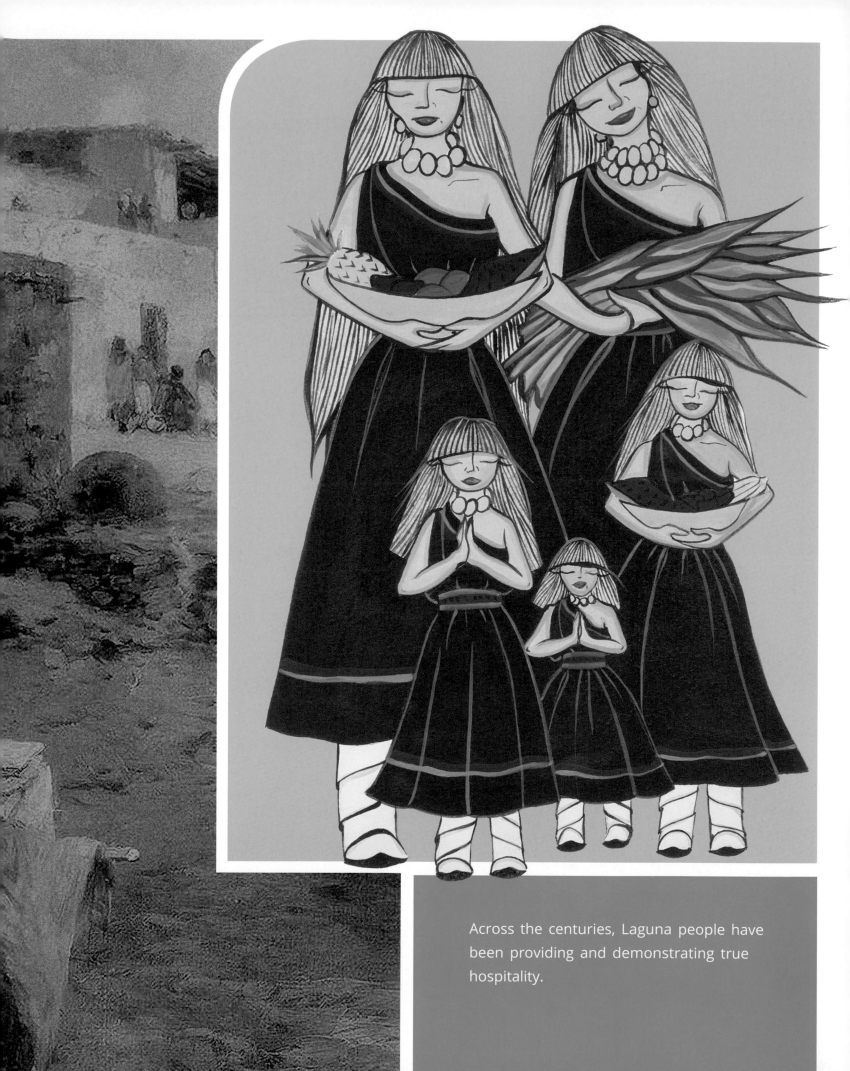

Across the centuries, Laguna people have been providing and demonstrating true hospitality.

THE CROSS ROADS.

For many decades, Laguna served as a crossroads for travelers moving across the desert. The natural location was defensible and yet, a visible feature for merchants, explorers, and visitors from other tribes. Laguna was a hub for trade and innovation throughout these decades.

A notable moment came in 1864, when the Navajo were forced on the Long Walk by the U.S. Government, wherein they were relocated from Eastern Arizona to Central New Mexico. Along the way, the Navajo marched through Laguna and, for a moment, were given some respite and care by the Laguna people.

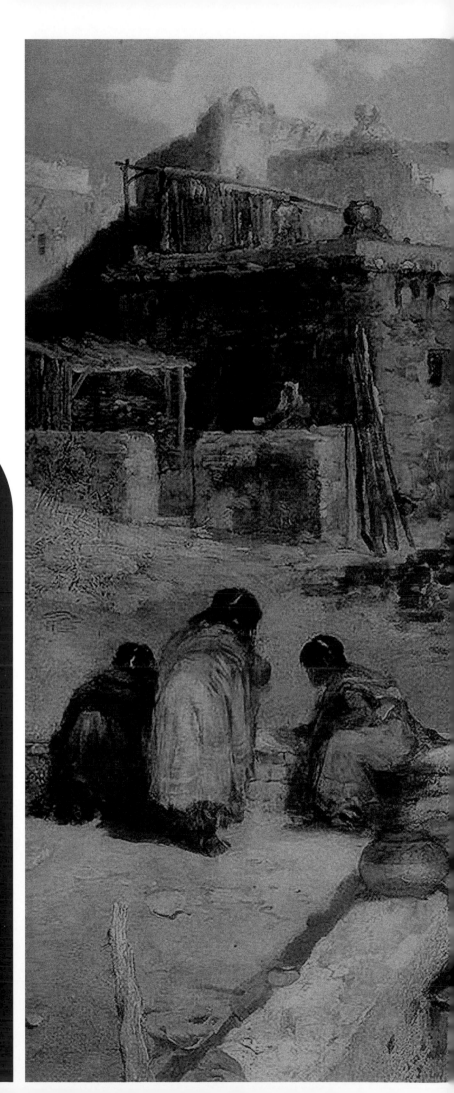

On August 10, 1680, after years of violence and oppression by the Spanish, the Pueblo people rose up.

They started a revolution never seen before in the world. Although there had been several actions of resistance before the Rebellion, the coordinated effort by all the Pueblos was sudden and stunning. In a matter of days, the Pueblos drove the Spanish back to the territory south of the Rio Grande River. The Pueblo people successfully kept the Spanish conquistadors back into New Spain (Mexico) for almost ten years.

The Pueblo of Laguna was not involved in direct conflict but served as a sanctuary for many Pueblo people who rightly feared retaliation from the Spanish government following the rebellion and violent reconquest ending in 1690. The arrival of these new Pueblo individuals and families grew the population of Laguna. This brought in new ideas and new innovations.

In 1699, the Catholic church of San José de la Laguna was completed. It formally established the Pueblo as part of the Spanish empire. Like many of the early churches in the Pueblos, it had been built with forced labor. Nonetheless, it became a symbol and eventual source of pride for the people of Laguna over the following centuries.

THE PUEBLO REBELLION

The Spanish brought with them new technologies and a new religion: Catholicism. The Laguna people were forced to assimilate. The Spanish were a colonial power. They viewed the Pueblo people as unequal subjects of their empire. As the Spanish grew more violent, the Pueblo people, including those at Laguna, realized something needed to be done.

HISTORY AT-A-GLANCE

Some stories tell of Laguna people migrating to arrive at their current home called Kawaik'a.

Their journey was long and filled with trials. But eventually, they settled in a place of canyons and incredible beauty. For many centuries, they lived a peaceful, farming life. They tended crops and built sustainable villages throughout the canyons and hillsides.

By the mid-1500's, the first Spanish colonizers noted this small group of people living near a naturally-dammed lake. At first, they believed them to be a group from the Pueblo of Acoma. But they soon came to realize that these people had settled the area as a separate group.

WASHINGTON

MONTANA

NORTH D

OREGON

IDAHO

SOUTH D

WYOMING

NEB

NEVADA

UTAH

COLORADO

CALIFORNIA

ARIZONA

NEW MEXICO

TEXAS

MEXICO

Here you can see the interior of the St. Joseph's church at Laguna Pueblo beside Route 66.

Ishkay Hanu, One People, is a guiding principle of the Pueblo of Laguna. Since its beginnings, the people and the place have continued to be a destination where creativity and culture, imagination and innovation, technology and tradition have built a strong and vibrant community.

TRAVELING TO

PUEBLO OF LAGUNA, NEW MEXICO

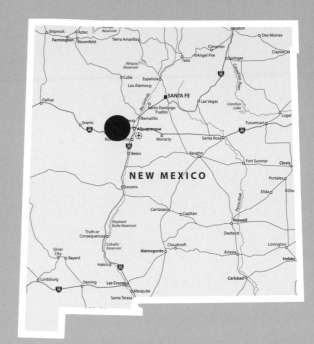

Where to Go

Visit the Rt. 66 Casino, Dancing Eagle, or the Laguna Superette where you can find great local food and fill up with gas.

Foods to Try

Laguna Pueblo is home to the award-winning and world-famous Laguna burger.

When to Go

Summer and Fall are the best times to visit. Check the Laguna Pueblo website to see which days are open to the public.

LOCATION

Forty-five miles west of Albuquerque, New Mexico sits the Pueblo of Laguna.

With a long and rich history and an even more exciting present, the Pueblo extends more than a half million acres. It's one of the largest reservations in the continental United States.

The Pueblo is made up of **six villages** and has almost 8,000 enrolled citizens. About half of them live within the boundaries of the reservation.

The history of the Pueblo is a history of **a unique place that has existed under four governments**. It continues today as an economic and cultural center-point for central/western New Mexico.

ROUTE 66

ONE LAND MANY NATIONS

PUEBLO OF LAGUNA

BY LEE FRANCIS IV
ILLUSTRATED BY
MICHELLE SISNEROS

Welcome to the PUEBLO OF LAGUNA

While many people think of the United States as one country and one land, it is actually a land made up of many nations.

Native American nations and pueblos currently exist in the lands called the United States.

And they've been here long before the United States became a country. These are sovereign nations and pueblos with their own laws. Their citizens have dual citizenship—in their nation or tribe and in the United States. These nations and pueblos have a rich history and culture that continues to today.

Let's learn about one of these, the Pueblo of Laguna, from a descendent of the Laguna people, Lee Francis IV.

Reycraft Books
55 Fifth Avenue
New York, NY 10003

Reycraftbooks.com

Reycraft Books is a trade imprint and trademark of Newmark Learning, LLC.
text © Reycraft Books

Educators and Librarians: Our books may be purchased in bulk
for promotional, educational, or business use. Please contact
sales@reycraftbooks.com.

Library of Congress Control Number 2021902056

ISBN: 978-1-4788-6814-9

Printed in Dongguan, China. 8557/0621/18090

10 9 8 7 6 5 4 3 2 1

First Edition Hardcover published by Reycraft Books 2021.

Reycraft Books and Newmark Learning, LLC, support diversity and
the First Amendment, and celebrate the right to read.